ADDRESS

BEFORE THE ALUMNI

OF

BOWDOIN COLLEGE,

JULY 8, 1873,

BY THE

REV. DANIEL R. GOODWIN, D.D., LL.D.,

PROFESSOR OF THEOLOGY

IN THE PHILADELPHIA DIVINITY SCHOOL.

BRUNSWICK:

JOSEPH GRIFFIN.

1873.

To the Rev. Daniel R. Goodwin, D.D., LL.D., Professor in the Philadelphia Divinity School.

Dear Sir:

At the meeting of the Association of the Alumni of Bowdoin College this day, it was

Voted, That the thanks of this Association be tendered to Professor Goodwin for his very able and interesting address delivered before them to-day, and a copy be requested for publication.

Respectfully yours,

J. B. Sewall, Secretary.

Brunswick, July 8, 1873.

Brunswick, July 10, 1873.

Professor Sewall,

Dear Sir, — The Address is cheerfully submitted to your discretion; in the hope that, as it has met with the kind approval of my brethren who heard it, its publication may be of service to the cause of right education.

Faithfully yours,

D. R. Goodwin.

The Rev. J. B. Sewall, A.M., Professor, etc.

BRETHREN, ALUMNI OF BOWDOIN COLLEGE:

By the invitation of your Committee, I come not to pronounce before you an oration, but simply to make a plain address. And the first duty of my office is the delightful one of welcoming you all once more, with myself, to the dear and sacred home of our common Alma Mater. I greet you all well — all brethren beloved, but especially near to me those for whom in former years I was permitted, after the Socratic fashion, to perform some part of the Lucinian office; or — varying the figure — to aid in the distribution to them of the wholesome and nutritious, though homely and perhaps at the time unsavory, diet which our provident foster mother furnishes from her carefully collected and well-kept stores.

But as I look around for the familiar faces and forms of those who were so long associated with me in this pleasing office, how changed, how blank the scene! That grand old sturdy Faculty with which Bowdoin College was so long identified — all gone, but one! One alone remains; like some giant pine of the primeval forest, spared by Boreas and the woodman's axe, still sound to the very core, with bark unscathed, lifting its solitary head, yet crowned with undiminished foliage, serene amidst the thrifty and aspiring trees of later growth that have vigorously shot up around. The rest, all gone; — some indeed transferred to other scenes of activity, or withdrawn to the quiet retirement and learned leisure which are so attractive to advancing years; but others, alas, how many, for us too many, translated to the world unseen. *Afflavit Deus et dissipantur.* All respected and honored as my teachers and fathers, they were afterwards esteemed and loved, with a ripened fraternal affection as my friends and colleagues.

There was the impassive, inflexible ALLEN, precise, stately, stiff; but just and kind and faithful; *antiqua homo virtute et fide;* more learned than apt to teach; a good ruler for all but the unruly. There is a maxim of college government emanating from the school of the celebrated and excellent Dr. Nott, which reads something like this: "Be sure you make friends of the scoundrels, you need have no fear from the good men"; or, in its earlier and naïve pagan version: "Keep on good terms with the Devil, and God will do you no harm." President Allen never adopted the detestable maxim. He never courted popularity; and so, perhaps, he never deserved it. With a warm and generous heart beating unseen and unsuspected beneath the cold exterior, living in all good conscience before God every day, he met abuse and obloquy with the invincible bravery of Christian meekness. Late he has gone to his rest.

There too was the gentle NEWMAN, the faithful friend, the classical scholar, the skillful and patient teacher, the accomplished Christian gentleman; — beautiful, delicate, pure as the opening flower of spring, he faded early from our sight; but he left the fragrance of a good man's name behind.

There was the magnificent and massive CLEAVELAND, *clarum et venerabile nomen, — totus, teres, atque rotundus,* — with stuff enough in him to make a dozen men; exuberant in intellectual power, in labor indefatigable, of eagle vision, masterly in construction, wise in selection, lucid in exposition, a true lover of science but an inveterate hater of theory; as a lecturer unequalled, as a teacher unsurpassed; the model professor, joining gravity and playfulness in one, making knowledge attractive, and study a delight; in government claiming severity as his own exclusive privilege, yet always shrinking from its actual exercise; forgetting nothing, remembering everybody; among the fathers and founders of the College, yet the genial brother of all her sons. He fell bravely in the harness; and never did college suffer a sorer bereavement. It is most fitting that old Massachusetts Hall, the original nucleus of the College, named from his native State, and the scene of his life-long labors should be re-fitted and replenished as his enduring memorial. Long may it stand, a monument consecrated by Bowdoin College to Professor Cleaveland!

There was the indomitable and uncompromising SMYTH; *justus, propositi tenax*, stern in principle, rough in exterior yet of finest sensibilities, a Great-heart in courage and in kindness, a Bayard in chivalrous sentiments, of more than feminine tenderness and delicacy, unselfish, uncalculating, often the best friend of those who took him for their enemy. To be first a man and then a gentleman, *esse quam videri*, was the motto of his life. He was a conscious enemy to no one. His was a fierce and fiery nature, but its intensest heats had their focus in the intellect and the conscience, in the clear apprehension and deep sense of right, and not in any violence of passion. His greatest fault was, that, born an enthusiast, he was made a professor of mathematics. I loved him, and trusted him, as my own dear friend. He loved his family with a peculiar strength of affection,— so he loved his friends, so he loved his Church, so he loved his country, and so he loved the College. Whatever he felt, he felt through and through; whatever he did, he did with all his might. The College had no more devoted and zealous servant or benefactor than Professor Smyth. For the College he lived; and for the College he died. Memorial Hall will not only perpetuate the memory of those noble sons of Bowdoin who fell in defence of their country, but of him, too, who no less nobly fell in laboring for its erection. Memorial Hall will be Professor Smyth's own monument. Let it speedily be finished. The *rudis, indigestaque moles* stands there now, a discredit indeed to the College, but no detraction from Professor Smyth. Its very incompleteness is eloquent of what in him the College lost.

There, too, was the sensitive and saintly UPHAM, who has but just passed away from his earthly labors;—half hermit, half man of the world; a most extraordinary combination of weakness and strength, of simplicity and astuteness, of bashful modesty and unflinching boldness; shrinking as the mimosa, not only from human touch but from the very gaze of human eyes, yet ready to march fearlessly to the cannon's mouth — in the dark; a poet, a philosopher, a philanthropist, a mystic, the very apostle of universal love; prolific in plans, exhaustless in expedients, in effort unwearied, as versatile and many sided as Ulysses, — πολυμήχανος, πολύτροπος, πολύμητις 'Οδυσσεύς, — but to the right and the good as steady at heart as the needle to the pole; often, perhaps habitually, driven by sheer modesty out of the straightforward high road into bypaths and circuitous ways. Of large and varied learning, and of the broadest human sympathies, genial and generous to a fault, he sought to find what was good in everybody, — even in the oddest and most anomalous specimens of human kind. He did as much as any man to give a high reputation to Bowdoin College. He knew no vacation when any work was to be done in her behalf, and that he might increase her endowment he impoverished himself. The Latin instruction should never have been imposed upon him; yet he made us read and learn more Latin than all the nice analyses and minute philosophies of the boasted modern critical method will ever, in the same time, instill into our successors. Upham, too, is gone.

Cleaveland, Smyth, Upham — I found them all professors here when, as a student, I entered College near fifty years ago. They continued at my side all the time I was a member of the Faculty, and here I left them all in full strength and activity just twenty years since. But now the eye seeks for them in vain. Forgive me that I have thus dwelt upon their memories. I could not speak here to-day and forbear to speak of them; and when I begin to speak of them I know not where to stop. To me the very air of the place is burdened with their presence. I never saw a Commencement here without them. In my thoughts they and the College are one. I not only knew them as most of you knew them — as honored and revered instructors — but I knew them more intimately and familiarly than did most of you, as colleagues, neighbors, friends. In their loss I feel a sense of personal bereavement. They were no ordinary men. They were men of mark; men of striking and noble traits; men of whom Bowdoin College has occasion to be proud.—They are gone; but far distant be the day when it shall be said that the places which once knew them know them no more. While Bowdoin College stands, their memories shall be perpetuated. *Fama semper vivat, viridisque floreat.*

First, then, let us lift our hearts in thankfulness to the good providence of Almighty God, which gave us such a mother—a mother associated with such men and such memories, and which has spared so many of us to stand together around her here today—here to rise up again and call her blessed.

Next, wasting no further word of preface, let us proceed at once to consider the subject which, before all others, the times and this occasion press upon our attention. You anticipate that I propose to speak of the proper function of the American college.

WHAT THE COLLEGE HAS TO DO, AND HOW TO DO IT.

"As to the Latin language, my son is not to learn it, and I will not even allow any one to speak to me any further on the subject." Such were the instructions of the great bear of Brandenburg for the education of his son, who afterwards became Frederic the Great. The Greek was not prohibited simply because the Greek was quite out of the question; and not only was the Latin language placed under the ban, but, in the same instructions, the same high authority declares that "the history of the Greeks and the Romans ought to be abolished; they are good for nothing." Of course the instructions were not followed; had they been, Frederic the Great would not have been what he was. In spite of the brutal father's ponderous and bloody cudgel, they were by some means or other evaded. But how wonderful the prophetic instinct, the anticipative vision of the great barbarian! How strange that the rough old Prussian king should, more than a century and a half ago, have so cleary reached, and been ready with the sturdiest blows of his heavy-headed cane to defend, the very same sage conclusion which the self-styled public opinion of this wise and enlightened age is with louder and louder vociferation, urging us to adopt!

When we of the old time came to college we thought a classical culture a desirable accomplishment, and we came that we might acquire it. Very few, I think, of those among us who faithfully pursued, and so—at least partially—achieved the work, have since changed their mind or repented their course. And such continued the prevailing sentiment during the whole period of my connection with the College. But now, after an absence of a score of years, I return to find the air resounding all over the land with the cry: "down with the Greek," "down with the classics," "down with the mathematics"; a cry which, like a north-east storm, has come drifting backward from the south and west, and has penetrated even to the heart of New England, until the President of the oldest University in the country is reported to have distinctly formulated the sentence for the entire abolition of *the Greek*, at least, from the course of studies required in college for the regular degrees. It is true the curriculum of the American college has all along included much besides the classics, or the classics and mathematics,—physics, philosophy, logic, rhetoric, sciences, arts, history, literature; and in our own college, for many years, the study of the French and German languages and literature has been wisely added; yet the basis and backbone of the whole was understood to be *classical culture.* Those other things have been gradually crowding upon this, and now, in the spirit of Frederic William, the demand is made that it be abolished altogether.

On this question, we propose to seek the ἀρίστον μετρὸν, the *juste milieu;* and, that we may more distinctly see where that lies, that we may better appreciate what the American college has to do, and how to it, we need to refresh our minds and memories with a few principles and historical facts.

As preliminary to our discussion, we must first distinguish education into fundamental or liberal, and special or professional. And then, premising that the proper business of the college is to give a fundamental and not a professional education,—(1) Our first principle or postulate is this: The best fundamental education is that which best trains and perfects the man, disciplining and developing his powers in the highest degree. Man's own perfection is the first end of a right education. Man may perform, and admirably perform, all the work of a machine, of a tool, of a special trade or profession;—but let us have *the man* first; let us not have a mere machine, or tool, or craftsman.

Now it is in action that man is perfected; it is by exercise his powers are developed. *But any scheme or institute for his education implies some selection or condensation of appropriate means; some special arrangement, combination or adaptation of exercises fitted to this specific end;*—otherwise he might go about his business from the start, and get his exercise and training as he went along. An educational institute must be a gymnasium,—not the workshop of any particular trade.

As language is at once the most characteristic product and the very organ of the human mind, the means and the measure of human culture, language must naturally furnish the most appropriate and effectual gymnastic for man's education. The study of language touches the mind at all points, and brings into play all its faculties. It offers an easy beginning with a gradual progress to severer efforts, and may be pushed till the powers are strained to their utmost tension. The classical languages and literature, from their peculiar structure; from their perfection of form; from their beauty of style; from their treasures and models of philosophy, poetry, history and eloquence; from their special radical connection with our own language and culture, with our history, religion, science, and all our civilization and modes of thought; furnish, as all experience conspires to teach, the most perfect gymnastic apparatus of all the languages we could select for study. The many sided exercise they afford needs only to be supplemented at some points by the more rigorous and exact methods of the mathematics, according as different minds are capable of grasping and pursuing them. And it is very rare that a good classical scholar is destitute of mathematical ability, or would fail to be profited by its exercise — an exercise whose utility, moreover, is often measured by its unpalatableness. This classical and mathematical discipline may next be fitly applied and further perfected by proceeding to the more abstract conceptions, the nicer analyses, the abstruser speculations, the more patient introversions of thought, the more subtle reasonings, as well as the profounder and more essential problems, of ethics and metaphysics;—where mental discipline reaches its highest goal.

We by no means ignore or disparage or undervalue the physical sciences, but we cannot regard their study as specially adapted for the general disciplinary purpose of a fundamental education. They are rather particular directions in which the mental powers, whether disciplined or undisciplined, may be applied; and some of them may be well and wisely attached to a collegiate curriculum, so far as room can be found for their study, as both a relief and an encouragement for severer discipline. Even in the pursuits of science the man of classical and mathematical culture has a vast advantage. We may appeal to any teacher who has had a class of young men to instruct in any branch of knowledge which required close attention and discrimination, whether he has not found a marked, an immense, difference between those who had had a previous training in the languages and those who had not, in respect to their power of mastering a complex subject. And to all teachers in professional schools we may appeal in like manner.

For one sort of discipline, indeed, the physical sciences may furnish the best means — that is, the discipline of observation by the senses. But this is the cheapest and lowest kind of all discipline. It is the discipline in which not the civilized but the savage man is most proficient. Yet it is not to be neglected or despised, but rather most earnestly insisted on, not so much for its comparative intrinsic importance, as because it is so apt by scholars and men of culture to be left quite out of the account. Add it to a scholastic discipline, and it is a vast improvement; substitute it for that discipline, and it is a sorry exchange — a child's whistle for the lyre of Apollo; a mess of pottage for the birthright of humanity. So far as the object is to accumulate external facts, to acquire a knowledge of nature, or a faculty for such acquisitions, observation and the habit of observation, the ever-ready, intent and sharpened eye and ear are of the highest moment. But this is not the discipline of the man. Man himself is a higher end than knowledge even — much higher than a knowledge of the external world.

In like manner, physical education may be of great importance, and may demand more attention than it has received in connection with our institutions of learning; yet few would fail to recognize the folly of *substituting* it for intellectual culture, even though they may have the high authority of Lycurgus for such a proceeding. More of a specifically *political* education, too, may be highly desirable, especially among us; but who, in his senses, would propose to *substitute* it for a classical and mathematical discipline?

And here I cannot help seriously raising the question, whether many of the most lauded improvements in the methods of modern education are not greatly missing the mark. In them the readiest mode of conveying knowledge, and not the arousing and sharpening of the mental powers, is the end; and in them the more perfectly everything can be represented to the external senses, and the less the powers of abstraction and intellectual elaboration are taxed, the better. Hence a multiplication of models and drawings, and a studied exuberance of striking, brilliant and amusing experiments. Hence the boasted invention of object teaching. This invention may be very well in infant schools, but to propose in this way to give a fundamental education is no better than to substitute for the exquisite poetry and history of Greece and Rome, and of our own modern culture, an improved edition of the hieroglyphics of Egypt, or of the pictorial writings of the Aztecs and the Winnebagoes. It tends to dwarf the mind; to give a distaste for real intellectual exertion; to paralyze the reflective and logical faculties. To those habituated to this training the classics naturally become an excrescence and the mathematics a bore. Let us not be misunderstood. This mode of instruction is of very great value, and to be very highly commended, in its proper place, — where the object is, not to train the mind, but simply to communicate knowledge, and to communicate it most easily and clearly. Then every simplification and illustration is an improvement. If not carried too far, or pursued too long or too exclusively, this mode of instruction may sometimes serve to arouse the excessively stupid to attention, inquiry and effort, and thus prepare the way for intellectual training. But to substitute it in the place of that training is to invert or abolish the whole idea of discipline; it is to thrust the rule of ordinary life — the rule of expending as little effort as possible in attaining what we desire — into the very process of education, where the precise object is to increase our powers of acquisition; it is to reap the harvest in the spring, or to eat up the seed that should be sown for a future crop. And yet it may be said, what is the wheat for but to be consumed? and the less that is wasted in the ground, is it not the better?

If it be thought that there is no need of an artificial accumulation of difficulties in the process of education simply to task and stretch the mind; that it will be tasked and stretched sufficiently in the process of ordinary acquisition, and after all possible helps and simplifications; — this is very plausible. But it simply abandons and repudiates the idea of a fundamental education, a preparatory discipline, an intellectual gymnasium altogether. Instead of laying the foundation within, it goes to seek the foundation without. Instead of disciplining the mind once for all, that it may be prepared for any study or business, it sets it at once about its business, that it may acquire its discipline as it goes. The instance of the mathematics will perfectly illustrate the whole case. According to this new method, the more the mathematics can be dispensed with the better; for the less of mathematics involved in it, the easier the study of any science, whether, for instance, of astronomy or of mechanics. The object is to reduce the mathematics to a minimum, and thus to restore astronomy to its primitive pastoral simplicity and mechanics to the rule of thumb. But on the other scheme, and according to our theory of education, the mathematics are to be used as a direct means and *organon* of intellectual discipline and development; and, within reasonable limits, the more mathematics, the more mathematical training acquired, the better — the better for the mind, the better for the other sciences. And so of the languages; — the languages are to be studied in their inward relations to the processes of thought; and not mere picture books to convey the clearest views of external objects. Suppose a person is to be directed how to go to a certain spot; it is one thing to give him a map of his way — and that is the surest thing, for with that he is a fool if he does not find it,—and it is another thing to describe accurately and vividly in words the track to be pursued. This latter requires much more intellectual power and training in him who skillfully gives the description, and vastly more in him who is able to apprehend and follow it. Yet this is the kind of intellectual power to which men need to be trained, even for the practical purposes of every day life. The word-painting, not only of a lofty poetic creation but of a masterly historical narrative or description, is, in my apprehension, of a higher order than even the most finished fancy or historical picture on the canvass. The creative and constructive imagination on the part of the writer is at least equal to that required of the painter; and the faculty of bodying forth the imagination in words, is at least of as high and noble a character as the power of mixing or applying colors for the same purpose. As to the reader, a higher faculty of reproductive imagination and a more cultured taste are required in him than in the beholder of the picture, if they both would appreciate and enjoy the work of art before them. The power of abstract thought, of distinct intellectual conception, of vivid imagination, a cultivated taste, nice and accurate mental analyses and discriminations, clear views and critical judgments of complicated subjects,—these are what we want as the results of a right fundamental education. It is culture *versus* the savage state. It is man *versus* nature. The study of language is the study of man—"the *humanities;*" and it is with good right that a fundamental education, such as we have endeavored to portray, has been called a *liberal education.* Its end is the perfecting of man himself, and not his preparation to be a serviceable slave, or a means to any other earthly end.

(2) Our next principle is this:—The best fundamental education is that which best fits a man to be a medium of higher culture and elevation to the community,—preparing him most perfectly for the exercise of all, and especially of the liberal, professions, and for the higher duties of social and civil, of industrial and political, life. The perfecting of civil society is, next to his own perfection, the end of the individual's education.

Social culture is not a process of spontaneous fermentation in the mass, but it is an organic development in which there are some members of higher order than others, or it is a grand forward march in which there must be leaders of various degrees. For the general cultivation of society nothing is more needed than a highly cultivated class who may direct the movement and aid the efforts of those below them; who may stimulate to emulous exertion and present a lofty pattern for imitation, and from whom the sweet influences of knowledge, culture, taste and refinement may descend, in gentle diffusion, through the whole mass. To furnish such an educated class is one of the functions of the American college; and we may proudly say, that in discharging this function, Bowdoin College has been pre-eminent. The graduates of no college have, in proportion to their numbers, done more than those of Bowdoin in the work of general education; have furnished more leading educators, more presidents and professors of other colleges, or more preceptors and teachers in the higher schools. Nor is this all; — no other college has, in proportion to the number of its alumni, furnished more men distinguished in the higher walks of polite literature; no other college can boast a Longfellow or a Hawthorne. Besides, in our highly educated class we intend to include not only teachers and authors, — those who make learning their profession, — but those, too, who carry the leaven of a liberal culture into all the varied pursuits and employments of practical life, whether of agriculture, commerce or manufactures.

But, particularly, a right fundamental education best prepares a man to exercise for the highest benefit of society what were once, more properly than now, called the learned and liberal professions. Who can doubt that the members of these professions have lost immensely; not so much, it may be, in the ability and success with which they discharge their strictly professional functions, as in their wholesome and elevating influence on the general culture of the community; since, among us, they have come to be so largely men who have never received a liberal education? Perhaps, even if it were possible, it would not be wise — and certainly it is not to be expected — that the former status should be restored, and that it should be here required by law, as in England and in Europe generally, that none should be permitted to enter upon the exercise, or to enjoy the honors and emoluments, of either of the learned professions, without having received a liberal education.

> "Facilis descensus Averni,
> "Sed revocare gradum, — * * *
> "Hoc opus, hic labor est."

What is done is done; and the remedy must now come, not from a change of the law, but from a reformed public opinion. The bar generally, and the clergy of some of the denominations, have sunk least below the old standard; but if, not only the lawyers and the clergy, but the immense number of the annual recruits to the medical profession were compelled by the demands of an enlightened public opinion to have the degree of Bachelor of Arts in order to be admitted to their final examinations, how soon would our college classes be filled; and what an unspeakable advantage it would eventually be, not perhaps to the technical skill or the pecuniary success of the members of the professions, but to their personal character and respectability, and, what is here chiefly to be regarded, to their influence upon the general tone of social sentiment and culture! Little to the purpose is the trite and flimsy objection, that many of the most distinguished jurists, physicians and divines, have been destitute of a collegiate training. Men may acquire a thorough education, a thorough classical and mathematical discipline or its equivalent, without going to college; but, either colleges are a gross blunder from beginning to end, or they offer the best opportunity for such an acquisition. Yet he has doubly made the acquisition who has made it by force of mere persistent energy and indomitable purpose, against all odds, without the usual helps, by snatches and intervals and working his way backward, contriving to support his partially erected superstructure while he places under it the foundation. Moreover, in some cases natural power and genius may be so great as to furnish the foundation itself, and need no fundamental discipline. It is the old antithesis of art and nature, as Cicero has put it; or education *versus* genius. Nature may do without art, but art cannot do without nature; genius may dispense with a regular education, but no education can ever produce genius. In comparing numbers it seems too often to be forgotten, that if of one thousand men only ten taken at random are sent to college, the chances are that there will be ninety-nine men of natural genius without a college education to one with it. The chance that such a genius as Shakespeare should have received a college training is not one in five hundred; — and yet Milton was a university man.

If a person would be distinguished in the walks of science, scientific wisdom would not suggest that his scientific training should be restricted to the pattern of that of Benjamin Franklin; nor would our mechanical engineers propose to keep the technical education of boys preparing for the profession of engineering within the limits of that of Arkwright or Fulton. And yet, with all their study and learning few of the boys can ever be expected to equal those great names.

We seek, not to create genius but to cultivate average ability. And that a thorough mental discipline and culture is in general a good thing for a man — both in his individual and social capacity, and especially as a preparation for the exercise of the liberal professions — is too plain to need further argument. The great trouble is the pitifully low aims, the miserable ideas of success, which fill the minds of men of all orders and degrees among us. Money, place, popularity, — these are the prizes. For these men strive; for these they live and die. But the empty pulpit declaimer fills his church and commands the largest salary; the coarse but cunning pettifogger fills his purse and goes to congress; the ignorant quack manufactures his new salve or pill and lives in his palace. How much of the social degradation and political corruption now alleged to be so fearfully rife among us is due to the low education of our professional men, and of those who climb to the highest places of honor and trust, may well be a matter of serious inquiry. They certainly seem to be greatest precisely in those States and in those parts of our country where the men who are put in high positions are more generally destitute of a college training. As an indication of the change that has come over us in this respect, it may be observed that of the first six Presidents of the United States four or five were, I believe, college graduates; while of the remaining twelve, only three or four had received a liberal education. That, on the other hand, the three or four *most* distinguished among them all should have been destitute of such an education, belongs to that class of facts which has just been explained. But, for the ordinary course of things, I verily believe that the generous discipline of a liberal education is one of the most important conservative and restorative influences on which we have to depend.

(3) Our third principle is this: — The best fundamental education is that which tends to keep the mind in its normal connection with the highest aims and objects of thought; and these lie in the moral sphere, and ultimately in that of religion. Religion is the golden chain that, let down from the battlements of heaven, binds man and all his strivings to the right centre — the throne of God.

From the earliest times, and among all historical nations, religion has presided over the education of mankind and the progress of human civilization. Thus we have not only the "medicine man" absorbing whatever there is of learning among the Africans and the North American Indians, but the magi holding the same position among the Chaldees and the Persians, the priests among the Egyptians, the schools of the prophets among the Hebrews, the Brahmins with their Vedas and Shastras, the Orphic Hymn to Jupiter, and the theogonies and mythologies of Hesiod and Homer with Thales and Pythagoras at the origin of the schools of Greek philosophy. The Greeks borrowed their philosophy and science from the priestly castes of Egypt and India, and were the first to secularize them, and it may be doubted whether, so doing, they ever greatly exceeded the measure of their masters. In process of time the Greek and Roman learning passed from heathendom to the Christian church. During the darkness of the middle ages, the monks and clergy preserved what of knowledge there was; and to be able to read and write was, until quite a recent period, the distinctive mark of a clergyman; whence came the very use and meaning of the modern terms "clerk" and "clerical," as well as of the old legal phrase "benefit of clergy." The church founded the great universities and colleges that marked the awakening of the European intellect from the long night of barbarism, that were both the cause and the effect of the revival of learning, and that have continued the grand centres of culture to the present day. To the church we owe the oldest, and indeed nearly all, of our American colleges.

Of late, objection has been made to the clergy's having so disproportionate a share in the function of education; and its secularization is demanded as a great reform. No doubt the priests or the clergy have sometimes abused their office, or been unequal to its adequate discharge; no doubt that, in these times, there are other classes of men quite as learned and quite as apt to teach as the clergy; no doubt the theological department absorbs too great a proportion of the endowments, in such a University as that of Oxford, where upwards of two-fifths of the whole emoluments are given in salaries to seven theological professors, against only three-fifths to thirty-three professors in all other departments. But, in this country, we have nothing of the sort; and, if we had, one extreme is not to be corrected by going to the other. Though in some respects the clergy have, from their peculiar character and training, a special fitness for the office of teaching, yet it is not essential that they should hold exclusive possession of that office, or even retain it at all. *But religion is essential.* In secularizing education the priests may be thrown out, if you will; provided you are honestly disposed to retain religion — the Christian religion; for, if *we* are to have any religion in the practical sense, it can be no other than the Christian religion. The instructors may be laymen or clergymen, it matters not; but religion must by all means be retained in its proper place, as the corner stone of the whole structure. No national culture without religion has yet been known; and it is to be hoped it never will be. Upon the whole character and tone of a generous fundamental discipline the influence of religion is most wholesome; indeed it is indispensable; it is like the sun with his light and heat and attraction in the midst of the planetary system. Religion is not learning, it is not science, it is not intellectual power; but, to all the elements of true culture, it is what charity is to all the Christian virtues, — "the bond of perfectness." It is the key note to all the varied rhythm and harmony of a right education. It is the leaven whereby the whole is leavened. Colleges and universities are to stand as bulwarks against the influx of sophistry and infidelity and popular delusions, on the one hand, and against bigotry, superstition and intolerance, on the other. With reference to this end, Bowdoin College is happily constituted; for, being under the control of one religious denomination, religious instruction can be given in a free and positive manner, without wrangling over it until it is reduced to the smallest modicum, as it must needs be in State institutions; as we have found with our Common Schools, and as Mr. Gladstone found, to his cost, with his Irish University. It only remains wisely and judiciously to use this opportunity in a frank, liberal and unsectarian, but earnest and Christian spirit, and the happiest results must be the consequence.

(4) Another characteristic of the best fundamental education is, that it best keeps up the connection of the present with the progress and attainments of the past. This historical continuity of human development is that which constitutes the most striking distinction between man and brute, and between man civilized and the savage; which belongs therefore to the perfecting both of man and of society, and without which religion would sink into African fetich worship, or dissolve into the fluctuating mirage of individual fancies, or explode to atoms in sporadic fanaticism.

It is sometimes said in disparagement of schools and colleges, that the great discoveries and inventions by which the advancement of science and the progress of society have been accelerated, have usually been made *out of* them rather than *in* them. In general it has been so; and from the nature of things it must be so. The function of colleges is, not to invent or discover new truths or facts, but to *train minds*, and to teach *what is given*, to *hand down* knowledge. This last is their *conservative function*, and it is a function of no small importance, — a conservatism which is the surest means and augury of true progress. No great state ever flourished without intellectual culture and schools of learning and philosophy — except Sparta; and that was only a nation, or rather a tribe, of robber athletes; and, what is still more remarkable, never were a people more doggedly and stupidly and fanatically conservative. Theirs was conservatism without growth or progress, and it ended, as such conservatism must end, in rottenness.

(5) Still another characteristic of the best system of education is, therefore, that it keeps abreast with the present advancement of knowledge and of society, in living sympathy with the spirit of progress, both stimulating and directing it. The college is to be the highest exponent of the best education and culture of the times, and the principal means of preserving, improving and propagating it. The college is both to hand down the torch and to prepare the ignitible material, which, upon the application of that torch, is to kindle into a new and increasing flame. The process is not a mere tradition; it is a propagation. All life is progressive; *the college must be progressive* or die.

The Grecian schools — Socratic, Platonic, Aristotelian, — were progressive rather than conservative; so much so as thereby to become exposed to popular obloquy. The science of law was the special form of knowledge added by the Roman mind to Grecian civilization. It survived the Roman Empire. It led to the foundation of the first mediæval university — that of Bologna. But theology resumed its historic rights in most of the other European universities, particularly in France and England.

I suppose we can form but an imperfect idea of the great stirring thoughts of the middle ages — theology, scholasticism, architecture and art — when students assembled by the twenty and thirty thousand at the universities of Paris and Oxford; and still less of the stupendous, enthusiastic, mental upheaving of the great revival of learning and free thought from 1450 to 1550. It was man standing in awe in the presence of nature's unfolding mysteries, and stirred to the profoundest depths of feeling and the highest intensity of intellectual activity by religious fervor and religious reform.

In comparison, modern times are common-place; because nature is now tamed and domesticated, and freedom of thought and belief is familiar. Man himself has now become more than all social organizations, — the masses more than any class. Man himself is now to be elevated, not palaces or cathedrals to be reared. The village school-house has a higher meaning, is a nobler monument, than the pyramid of Cheops. The Greek who first got his letters is remembered with gratitude and honor, while the names of those Egyptian kings who built the pyramids were held by their people in utter detestation. Cadmus will not be forgotten while Greek literature remains; and Greek literature will outlast the pyramids. Euclid, the schoolmaster of geometry, is immortal; but the tower of Babel with the names of all its builders has perished forever. Plato and Aristotle have inscribed their names on the walls of a temple which will crumble only when all sublunary things shall crumble. The simple writings of St. John and St. Paul, though ever so common-place, and though as familiar to children as household words, will survive all the grandest cathedrals that were ever built, — will continue to diffuse their gentle and life-giving beams until all human knowledge shall pass away in the blazing light of heavenly intuition.

The original Israelitish or Mosaic idea of society was that of a free people organized in families under the government of God. The oriental idea made the king everything and the people nothing, except so far as they might serve the king. Eventually the Israelites and Jews engrafted this idea upon their theocracy, or rather substituted the former for the latter. The Grecian idea elevated a class, was essentially aristocratic; this was the governing class — the citizens; the rest were slaves. The Romans, beginning with the Greek idea, endeavored to combine all these elements into one complex organization. The feudal system was an awkward and clumsy engrafting of the oriental upon the Greek idea, adopting also, in the papacy, a sham theocracy — an audacious caricature and perversion of the Mosaic idea — a caricature which had also appeared in Tartary in the form of Grand Lamaism. *Our* idea of the State is, that it is a divine institution for the highest good of all its members — its government to be "of the people, by the people, for the people."

In comparison with the Platonic or the Aristotelian philosophy, the Christian religion and Christ's teaching may be considered common-placc. The common people heard him gladly. Plato said that it was impossible to convey the knowledge of God to the common mind; but Christ has revealed it to babes.

Such is the teaching, such is the social condition, such are the ideas and aims, and such the means of accomplishing them, with which we have to deal. Such are the times in which our colleges are called to exercise their function; they must take the times as they are; and we have no reason to regret that they are such as they are. Wc must sympathize with the common people and seek to elevate them. We must sympathize with common-places and endeavor to arouse an interest in them; we must excite an enthusiasm for common-places, in view of their great underlying ideas. Surely no work can be grander than the culture and elevation of human kind.

The actual enthusiasm of the leading intellects at the present day lies in the direction of the physical sciences. We must recognize that fact, and, instead of struggling against it, must turn it to account. What it is reasonable to do at any time is imperatively demanded at the present juncture, — that we should seriously inquire whether the college curriculum may not need some modifications to adapt it to the state of the times. Living in the midst of changes we must constantly re-adjust our bearings. The divine revelation, in its successive utterances, was variously adapted to successive times. Preaching, too, must change, in its rhetoric, tone, and subsidiary themes, with the changing tastes and mental habits of different people and different ages. Bossuet's or Massillon's masterly discourses; Latimer's or Bunyan's or South's sermons, might not effect now what they did once. Even St. Paul's might receive further modifications were he to deliver them now;—he made himself all things to all men. Whitefield's fervent oratory might now fall flat; and it is questionable whether Chatham's style of eloquence, if reproduced, would secure a man weight or even a hearing in the British Parliament at the present day. According to the judicious Hooker, laws, even divine laws, may be changed, not only when their subject matter, the end to be accomplished by them, ceases, but when their object matter, the character or condition of the parties on whom they are to act, changes.

Colleges and universities *have* changed. The ancient Greek schools were chiefly philosophical and rhetorical. Grammar and mathematics must have been taught in a more private way—not in any great public institutions. The Saracenic and Mahometan schools of the middle ages were chiefly medical, mathematical and metaphysical. The early European universities were chiefly legal, theological and philosophical or scholastic. Letters were taught, but in a subordinate curriculum. The leading departments in the modern English universities are the theological, mathematical and classical; in the German universities, scientific, philosophical and professional—the mathematics and classics being the business of the gymnasia, but required for degrees in the universities. The American college was at first ecclesiastical, but always with a classical and mathematical curriculum. The present American colleges are in a transition state—partly gymnasia, partly universities, partly schools of science.

Thus we see that the great schools of learning have changed in their constitution and character from age to age. We should not think it good now to restore the *trivium* and *quadrivium;* why then should we suppose that precisely the form reached one or two hundred years ago, or which has been reached just now, is the best possible, and ought not to be further changed? All human works are susceptible of improvement and progress. The

Divine revelation alone is now once for all complete. If any human institution is thus perfect, can we show precisely when it became so, and why it must have become so just then, whether at its first start or at what subsequent period? Does the best always come first? And are mankind advancing in folly from generation to generation? If not, then may our collegiate systems be susceptible of improvement, and, still more, of enlargement. The college has always had two offices, the conservative and the progressive. These must remain united. The college is to lead the people; but it must be with the people in order to lead them. It is to be an exponent of the spirit of the times, — to restrain and direct by *leading on*, not by a reluctant dragging behind. This is at once true conservatism and true progress. Humdrum conservatism and humbug progressivism are alike to be eschewed. Universities when most flourishing have always been in sympathy with the leading intellectual tendencies of their age. The living instincts of humanity are more to be relied upon than any cut-and-dried theories. The office of the university is to connect the past and the future through the present, to guard against extremes and extravagances, to encourage generous and comprehensive views. But the grand function of the college is, as we have seen, to train and develop the man *as man*, and not as some particular machine; — it is discipline, culture. Now the appropriate processes for such a culture may vary with the times and the leading aims of human life at the given period. But classical culture will always be important and necessary until our very civilization changes its character. Other modes of culture may be connected with it, and, for individual cases, allowed to a large extent to be substituted for it, as the wants or demands of the age may suggest. Something like this must be done, or our colleges must surrender their traditional position at the head of the progress and culture of the times.

But these changes must be made with caution. They must not be revolutions, or total substitutions, but incidental modifications and chiefly *additions*. Additions may be safely made to almost any extent. Besides the fundamental education — always to be retained in its place and in its integrity — other special branches may be conjoined or subjoined, as means may be provided. Scientific and professional departments may be added to the courses of instruction, just as fast as provision is made for their endowment and support. And the readiness of the friends of the college, or of those who are zealous for its reform and improvement in this direction, to furnish such endowments, must be the practical measure of the public demand for the introduction of such reforms. The "demand" is not measured by the wish to have, but by the willingness and ability to pay. To transfer to these departments the funds and provision made already for the old classical and mathematical curriculum, would be hardly short of a breach of trust. In my own view it is extremely desirable that such new endowments should be made. A full course of scientific and technological, as well as of professional instruction, must be added to our college work; — the college must be raised to something of the character of the University, or, as matters are now going, must be content with the subordinate position of the classical school, or of the German gymnasium. And perhaps it is rather our pride than our wisdom that would shrink from such a result. For, classical schools and gymnasia, or their equivalents, we must needs have.

The old function of the college proper will always be required. If our colleges were at once all transformed into German universities, we should need, and we should soon establish in their place our old colleges, or the German gymnasia, to perform what would thus be abandoned of their present office — a fundamental general training, the preparation of a generous, liberal, classical culture, the proper discipline of humanity. This would be needed for the professions, too, especially for that of the clergy. And as regards science itself, it will always be found that no minds are so well prepared to grasp and pursue the properly *scientific* character and bearings of what is presented even in the popular lecture, as those which have been disciplined by a thorough classical and mathematical training. To see the scientific aspect, and to appreciate the scientific value of the brilliant experiment or of the newly discovered fact, requires other eyes than those of the body, and other helps to vision than that of the microscope. The most magnificent experiments may be enthusiastically gazed at, and yet convey no more scientific knowledge or culture than the changing views of the kaleidoscope. They may be no more than mere playthings for children.

Whenever and wherever, therefore, such additions as have been referred to are made, the classical course must be left intact; and the different academical degrees should honestly indicate what the graduate has accomplished, or, at least, what course of study he has pursued. If a man chooses to pursue a scientific rather than a classical course of study, why should he claim or desire the degree of Bachelor of Arts? Why not be satisfied with the honest and honorable designation of Bachelor of Science? To give the degree of B. A. to persons who have scarcely if at all pursued, or professed to pursue the study of Latin and Greek, is to utter a falsehood. The truth is, so far as that degree is an object of ambition or desire, it makes these two things clear: (1) that it should be given only to those to whom it belongs according to its proper meaning and significance; and (2) it shows that a classical training, or, at least, the credit of having received it, must after all be held highly desirable in the popular esteem; otherwise why should those who have not been willing to earn its degree be ambitious of adorning their names with its appropriate designation?

Let Bowdoin College be enlarged, then, without stint. She can never furnish too much provision for scientific or professional culture. There is no hostility or collision, or even incompatibility of temper, between science and the classics. There is room for nothing but mutual respect and friendship, or generous rivalry. Science and a taste for science cannot be annihilated; neither can classical learning nor a taste for classical learning be annihilated. Poetry and mathematics are alike indestructible. We need have

no fears of science. If there be any folly greater than the pretended antithesis of science and religion, it is that other folly of the antithesis of science and classical learning. Let both go on together, each helping instead of hindering the other. Let us propose no such miserable alternatives as learning *or* science, science *or* religion; rather let our watchword and battle-cry be — learning *and* science, science *and* religion, " now and forever, one and inseparable."

But let us remember not to expect too much from the college, however enlarged and reformed. No college can stand now where colleges used to stand. There are other agencies now in the field, which were scarcely known two hundred years ago — the press, teeming with its multitudinous books and pamphlets and periodicals and daily sheets, the common school, the high school, the technological school, popular lectures, — all sharing in the work which the college used to have to do almost alone — the work of shaping the character and culture, such as they may be, of the passing and the coming age. Still the peculiar function of the college was never more needed than just under these circumstances. Without the college and the education the college is designed to give, there is great danger that our whole intellectual culture should, both in its scope and character, degenerate and dwindle down to the limits of mere newspaper literature. Next to the Christian church the college must be, under God, the means of saving our civilization from shipwreck, from the return of utter barbarism, or from the universal prevalence of a shallow and vain-glorious spirit of vulgarity worse than barbarism itself.

The past of Bowdoin College is secure. The present is full of good auguries and glorious promise — the *auspicium melioris ævi.* With a faculty of rare ability and learning — a large proportion of whom I proudly look upon not only as brothers but as sons; with a President of devoted zeal and indomitable energy and consummate manliness, conjoined with the wisdom and prudence of a great leader, whose character and history command spontaneous respect, — CHAMBERLAIN, the scholar, the hero and

the statesman, — whose name, whether with the prefix of General, Governor or President, or with no prefix at all, should be pronounced only *capite aperto;* and with the efforts and arrangements that are now in progress for the enlargement of her endowments as well as of her apparatus and sphere of instruction, — sacrificing nothing of the old and gaining all of the new, — I rejoice, with you, to salute our dear old Alma Mater again; with you to bid her Godspeed on her mission of increasing usefulness.

www.ingramcontent.com/pod-product-compliance
Lightning Source LLC
LaVergne TN
LVHW020741120826
845150LV00010B/2288